W9-BSV-399

JAN    2005

# Great White Sharks

## ANIMAL PREDATORS

## SANDRA MARKLE

Carolrhoda Books, Inc. / Minneapolis

# THE ANIMAL WORLD IS FULL OF
# PREDATORS.

Predators are the hunters who find, catch, and eat other animals—their prey—in order to survive. Every environment has its chain of hunters. The smaller, slower, less able predators become prey for the bigger, faster, more cunning hunters.

And everywhere, there are just a few kinds of predators at the top of the food chain.

*In the oceans of the world, one of these is the great white shark.*

*A big female swims along* about 20 to 30 feet (6 to 9 meters) below the surface of the ocean, searching for prey. Her white belly lets her sneak up on prey looking up from deeper water toward the light of the sky. Her dark blue gray back keeps her camouflaged (hidden) as she slips up on prey looking down into the dark ocean depths from near the surface.

All of the great white's senses are alert for clues that could mean prey is nearby. This time, her sense of hearing provides the first clue. The shark has small ear openings on top of her head. These lead through canals to special sound-detecting sacs that send messages to the shark's brain. Distant clicks and high-pitched trills make the great white curious enough to change course and investigate.

Soon the great white female picks up a scent trail. The shark's nostrils aren't for breathing. They lead into nasal sacs packed with special scent-sensitive cells. Swimming forces water through the nostrils and into the nasal sacs. When the scent-sensitive cells detect chemicals in the water, they send messages to the brain. Then the hunter recognizes the scent as that of one of her favorite prey animals—seals.

The seals are unaware that a predator is approaching. They are playing it safe by staying in a group. That means there are lots of eyes and ears on the alert for hunters. It also means any approaching predators will have a harder time picking one animal to attack.

When the great white is about four car lengths away, she sees her prey. Even better, she spots one seal that's alone. Using powerful side-to-side sweeps of her tail fin, the great white female takes aim and surges forward.

Swimming fast, the female great white shark races toward the surface. Just before she reaches her prey, she opens her mouth. Both her upper and lower jaws are movable. She shoves them both forward, greatly increasing the size of her mouth opening. Armed with nearly one hundred teeth, she's ready to attack.

And what weapons these are! Each 2-inch (5-centimeter) tooth is razor sharp and has a serrated (ragged) edge to slice through tough skin.

*Just in time, though, the seal looks down and spots the hunter.*
The seal leaps, twisting in midair. The great white shark explodes from the water, snapping her jaws shut. But she's a fraction of a second too slow to catch the seal.

As the big female closed her jaws, two loose teeth fell out. That isn't unusual, though. The great white shark regularly sheds teeth, and new ones are continually developing inside her jaws. That way the hunter always has a set of strong, sharp teeth. Of course, before she can use these weapons, the great white female has to catch her prey.

*The great white shark is 16 feet (5 meters) long* and as heavy as a large car. Even so, she is able to hurl herself out of the water. Then she is able to twist her muscular body to turn in midair. As the seal plunges in and out of the waves, the big shark follows. When she's close enough to try another bite, she lunges, opening her big jaws and then snapping them shut again. This time, the hunter's teeth strike her prey's side. But the seal is young and quick. It surges forward at the right moment to just barely escape again. The shark's teeth only graze the seal's side.

*The seal is lucky.* The shark just missed biting off one of its hind flippers. These are what the seal uses to move itself through the water. If its flippers had been disabled, the shark could have finished off the seal easily.

With a burst of speed, the seal swims into water too shallow for the shark to follow. Then it leaps to safety on the rocky shore and waddles away from the water, leaving a line of blood trailing after it. Some of the seals watching the wounded youngster have scars from their own encounters with sharks.

*The great white is a predator that usually hunts alone.* So the only food the female gets to eat is what she catches herself. The shark immediately begins hunting again. She swims toward another group of seals. At the sight of the approaching shark, the seals crowd together. They struggle to keep behind the shark's head and away from her deadly jaws.

When the great white female turns and charges, two younger seals leap out of the water. Swimming fast, they easily escape, but an older seal lags behind.

Focusing on this prey, the great white surges forward and attacks. The seal leaps, but it's not as quick as the younger seals.

As she bites, the shark's eyes roll back to protect them from the struggles of her prey.  But the old seal barely wiggles before the shark's teeth stab into its middle, killing it.

Then, because the shark's teeth are designed for biting, not chewing, the great white female shakes her head to rip off a chunk of flesh. After she gulps this down, she rips off another bite and repeats the process until she's eaten her meal. Then she swims on.

*The muscle action needed for hunting* and to move the great white through the water creates heat. The great white shark is a fish. But unlike most other fish, sharks do not completely lose their body heat as they move. The shark's body is able to save some of its heat. This heat is circulated to help keep the shark's eyes, brain, and muscles working well even when the surrounding water is very cold. The big shark can respond and move faster than other, colder animals—an advantage when hunting in cold water. The shark's body also makes efficient use of the energy it gets from its food. So after eating a large seal, the great white may go as long as two months before she needs to eat again.

*The shark's big size* helps her catch big prey. But it also means she moves more slowly than when she was younger and smaller. So she's less likely to catch small, fast prey. She's definitely too slow to catch the small fish in this fast-swimming school. She swims on without wasting any effort trying. Even when she isn't hunting, though, the great white shark keeps on swimming. Bony fish, such as herring and cod, have a gas-filled sac to help them stay afloat. The shark does not have this sac. So the great white has to keep moving to avoid sinking.

Swimming also pushes water through the shark's mouth, past her gills, and out the slits in her sides. The gills, shown below, are actually pouches containing lots of balloonlike parts. As the shark's heart pumps, blood flows into and out of these gills. Oxygen from the water passes through the walls of the pouches into the blood. This oxygen-rich blood flows back to the heart and is pumped throughout the shark's body. Then the oxygen combines with nutrients from food the shark has eaten, giving the great white the energy she needs to live and hunt.

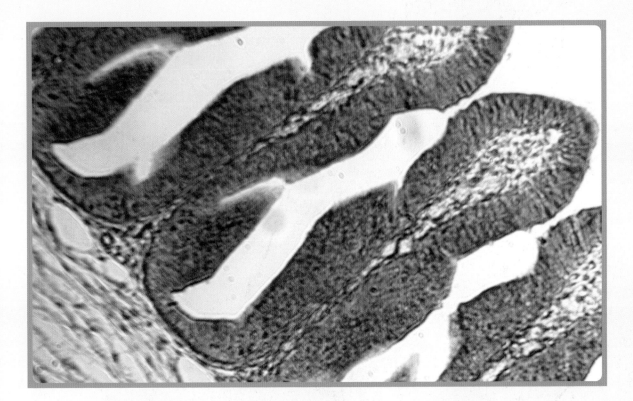

*The great white shark is especially attracted to the scent of blood* in the water. This time, an odor trail leads her to the floating body of a dead Bryde's whale. The great white will eat dead prey when she has a chance, so she digs in. After a while, another great white shark swims up and begins to feed from another part of the dead whale. Neither shark attacks the other. Great white sharks rarely fight. They avoid injury this way. So the big female feeds until she has eaten her fill. Then she swims away.

Another time, the great white female follows a blood trail to a wounded seal and quickly makes the kill. Such opportunities provide easy meals for the shark. By eating dead and dying animals, the shark also helps keep the ocean clean.

*Like most great whites,* the female prefers to stay in coastal waters. That's where she easily finds prey to ambush (attack). Day after day, the big female keeps on traveling and hunting. At the same time, something amazing is happening inside her big body. The shark is pregnant. Seven baby sharks, called pups, are developing. The female shark's body does not supply the pups with food. Instead, each pup has an attached yolk sac containing stored food. To get even more food energy while inside their mother, some great white pups will eat some of their brothers and sisters.

*When it's time for the pups to be born,* the surviving youngsters come out, one at a time, tail first. From the moment they leave their mother's body, the young great whites have to fend for themselves. But they're ready. Each youngster is already about 5 feet (1.5 meters) long and armed with a mouthful of sharp teeth.

At first, the young great whites will prey only on smaller fish. They will also have to be on the alert for bigger sharks that might attack them. Year after year, the young great whites will get bigger. And, in time, they will take their place among the top predators hunting in the world's oceans.

# Looking Back

- Look at the shark's tail on any page where you can see its whole body. You'll discover that the upper half of the tail is longer than the bottom half. When the shark moves its tail to turn, the longer upper part digs into the water more deeply than the lower part. And that helps the shark make its turns faster.

- Take a really close look at the shark's teeth on page 11. If you could touch a great white shark, you'd discover that its whole body is covered with little toothlike scales. This rough coat is like armor. It also traps a layer of water around the shark so its body moves through the water more easily.

- Turn back to page 19 and one of the first things you'll see is the great white's tall dorsal fin. While this shows the hunter's location, it also keeps the shark steady and on course. Without this fin, instead of moving forward, the shark would roll over with each side-to-side sweep of its tail.

# Glossary

BLOOD: the fluid that carries nutrients and oxygen to all body parts and carries away wastes, including carbon dioxide

BRAIN: the body part that receives messages about what is happening inside and outside the body and controls the response

GILL: a body part that allows the shark to breathe. Oxygen is taken in through the gills, and carbon dioxide is released into the water.

NASAL SAC: the body part lined with cells to detect scents and send messages to the brain

NOSTRIL: the opening leading into the nasal sac

NUTRIENTS: the chemicals food is broken down into for use by the shark's body

OXYGEN: a gas in the air and water that is passed into the blood in the gills and carried throughout the shark's body. Oxygen is combined with food nutrients to produce energy for the shark.

PREDATOR: an animal that is a hunter

PREY: an animal that a predator catches to eat

PUP: a young shark

TOOTH: a hard body part sharks use for grabbing and tearing at food. New teeth are developing all the time to replace teeth that are lost.

YOLK SAC: a stored food supply for developing young

# Further Information

## Books

Berman, Ruth. *Sharks.* Photographs by Jeffrey Rotman. Minneapolis: Carolrhoda Books Inc., 1995. The natural history of sharks is told in text and photographs.

Brennen, Joseph K. *The Great White Shark.* New York: Workman Publishing Company, 1996. This book, accompanied by a reproduction of the American Museum of Natural History's diorama, lets readers discover how the shark is successful in its environment.

Cerullo, Mary, and Jeffrey Rotman. *The Truth about Great White Sharks.* San Francisco: Chronicle Books, 2000. This book describes the shark's physical traits, the difficulties scientists have studying great whites, and the animal's potential to provide medical benefits for people.

Levine, Marie, Karen Dudley, and Patricia Miller-Schroeder. *Great White Sharks.* Austin, TX: Raintree / Steck-Vaughn, 1998. This book reveals the truth about great white shark myths and describes research into this shark's history.

## Videos

*National Geographic's Great White Shark: Truth about the Legend* (National Geographic, 2000). *Jaws* author Peter Benchley teams with noted underwater photographer David Doubilet to report on the reality of this shark's interactions with people.

*The Sharks* (National Geographic, 1982). This video investigates all kinds of sharks and includes lots of underwater footage.

# Index

*With love, for dear friends, John and Barbara Clampet*

The author would like to thank Dr. John E. McCosker, Senior Scientist and Chairman, Department of Aquatic Biology, California Academy of Sciences, and Dan Godoy, Marine Scientist for Kelly Tarlton's Antarctic Encounter and Underwater World, for sharing their expertise and enthusiasm. As always, a special thanks to Skip Jeffery, for his help and support.

## Photo Acknowledgments

The images in this book are used with permission of: © James D. Watt / Seapics.com, p. 1; © Ron & Valerie Taylor / Seapics.com, p. 3; © Jonathan Bird / Seapics.com, p. 4; © Ralph A. Clevenger / CORBIS, p. 7; © Ingrid Visser / Seapics.com, p. 8; © Tobias Bernhard / Oxford Scientific Films, p. 9; © Marilyn & Maris Kazmers / Seapics.com, pp. 10, 21, 23; © Doug Perrine / Seapics.com, pp. 11, 19, 32; © C & M Fallows / Seapics.com. pp. 12, 15, 16, 22, © Ralf Kiefner / Seapics.com, pp. 20, 31; © David Fleetham / Oxford Scientific Films, pp. 24, 28, 35; © Jeff Rotman / Seapics.com, p. 27; © Ron Boardman; Frank Lane Picture Agency / CORBIS, p. 29; © David B. Fleetham / Seapics.com, p. 36.
Cover: © David B. Fleetham / Seapics.com
Back cover: © Ron & Valerie Taylor / Seapics.com

Carolrhoda Books, Inc.
A division of Lerner Publishing Group
241 First Avenue North
Minneapolis, MN 55401

Website address: www.lernerbooks.com

Library of Congress Cataloging-in-Publication Data

Markle, Sandra.
    Great white sharks / by Sandra Markle.
       p.   cm. — (Animal predators)
    Includes bibliographical references (p.  ) and index.
    ISBN: 1—57505—731—X (lib. bdg. : alk. paper)
    ISBN: 1—57505—747—6 (pbk. : alk. paper)
    1. White shark—Juvenile literature. [1. White shark. 2. Sharks.] I. Title.
    QL638.95.L3M365 2004
    597.3'3—dc22                                        2003023180

Manufactured in the United States of America
1 2 3 4 5 6 — DP — 09 08 07 06 05 04